Starting Your North Carolina Corporation

Richard Wayne Bobholz

ISBN-10: 0-9977338-3-7
ISBN-13: 978-0-9977338-3-9

DEDICATION

This book is dedicated to those strategic partners of Law++ that have helped our clients through their non-legal needs. We truly appreciate the dedication you put forth when handling the referrals we make. Our word is on the line when we refer to you, and we're constantly impressed by how you handle their needs. Thank you.

CONTENTS

INTRODUCTION

If you're reading this, you're likely planning on forming a North Carolina Corporation. I'm very excited for you, as that's a huge step in starting your own company.

I got into the business of law because I enjoy helping other people start their companies and maintain them in a safe way. To that end, this book aims to help even more people than I can in my day-to-day. If you have questions above and beyond what this book can answer, please feel free to reach out to me at richard@lawplusplus.com. I'll answer whatever I can, but be aware that I receive hundreds of emails every day, and it may be a few days before I can reply.

As we lawyers do, I must also give you a couple of disclaimers. First of all, all the information in this book is educational and informational in nature. Because I do not know your specific facts, I cannot give you any sort of legal advice, and this book should not be taken as such.

Secondly, nothing written in this book is meant to establish an attorney-client relationship. I'd be more than happy to discuss that possibility, but there is no relationship of that nature until an engagement letter is signed by both you and I. Even if I handed you this book and said "this is exactly what you need," that should not be taken as representation.

Thirdly, if you do choose to contact me, please keep the inquires specific as to who you are, but general about all other facts. This is because we have conflicts of interest and I must ensure that I do not gain information from you that could help or harm one of my current clients. Here's an example:

Hi Richard. My name is Benjamin Franklin. I'm starting a print shop and library called "The Electric Key" and I was hoping to talk with you about copyrighting my works of literature. Can you help with that? Thank you, Ben.

Lastly, laws change, circumstances change, and your situation is likely unique. Because of this, I cannot guarantee everything in this book will be useful (or even not harmful) in your situation. I know you're a smart person and can use independent judgment when deciding what is right for your situation.

About Law Plus Plus

Law Plus Plus is an innovative law firm where we analyze the best way to operate a law firm for the benefit of our business clients. Our analysis has lead us to the creation of almost 100% flat rate fees, easy to understand policies, monthly subscriptions, business development help, and much more.

For more on Law++, check out www.lawplusplus.com.

Questions? Comments? Feedback? Requests for Other Books? Motivational stories? Feel free to email me at richard@lawplusplus.com.

CHAPTER 1
CHOICE OF ENTITY

Starting a company is a lot of work, I know, but when you put all the work in, it's worth it in the end. Let's get into the different options you have when considering choice of entity for your new business.

At this point in your startup process, I'm assuming you've got some sort of plan. You know where this venture is headed, and you know what your goals are. Whatever your goals, at this point, it is vital to have them.

Before we start, always remember that if set up properly, it isn't that difficult to switch between entity types, but it will cost you a minimum of the state filing fee for a new entity, plus whatever other expenses you'll incur. Keep that in mind as we move forward.

There are six main choices for for-profit entity type:

1. Sole Proprietorship
2. Partnership
3. Limited Partnership
4. Limited Liability Company (LLC)
5. S Corporation
6. C Corporation

You've probably heard of a few, if not all of these. I've placed them in this order because it is how I view the spectrum of liability and formality. I start at the top and decide if that is an appropriate fit or not. If it isn't, I move to the next, stopping only when I feel it is an appropriate structure for the company I am about to start. We will do the same here.

Sole Proprietorship

This is what you have if you just start a business, by yourself, without filing any papers with the state. There's no filing requirement outside of any necessary business licenses for specific business activities. There is also no additional tax or tax formalities. Certain ordinary business deductions can be made on your personal 1040 and all revenue is reported as wages. In North Carolina, these earnings and deductions would be reported on your D-400 tax form.

As a sole proprietor, you must also pay your self-employment tax, which includes both halves of the FICA tax. In 2012, this rate is 13.3% of your income, normally 15.3%. You are entitled to a deduction on your income taxes for the 7.65% of the FICA that is attributed to the business side.

What is most concerning about sole proprietorships is the fact that they subject the owner to unlimited liability. Because the business and the owner are one in the same, any debts or wrongdoings of the company are debts and wrongdoings of the owner. Even with an otherwise amazing asset protection plan, this is not a good position to be in unless you're 100% certain you and your company will not get sued.

Partnership

Also called a general partnership, this is the entity that is formed when you start a business with multiple people as owners with no entity filed with the state. Partnerships require no filings upon formation or annual reports, but would still require any business license to be obtained.

General partnerships are owned and controlled equally by each partner, absent an agreement that stated otherwise. Because any one partner can control the company and make it do whatever that partner wants, it is very important to have a partnership agreement in place before starting the company. Also, partnerships are merely a collection of people, meaning that the partnership of Bobholz, O'Brien and Smith is just the collective efforts of Bobholz, O'Brien and Smith. If Smith were to pass away, the partnership would die with him. What each partner owns is an equal share of the assets and profits of the company. There's no stock, nor any way to sell a partnership share.

As mentioned, partnerships should have partnership agreements prior to engaging in business together. This is a document agreed upon by all the partners that outlines how the company is to be run, how ownership is distributed, how earnings are distributed, and all the other very important details that should be discussed prior to entering into a partnership. Absent a partnership agreement, the terms are determined by the default rules in the North Carolina Uniform Partnership Act under Chapter 59 of the North Carolina General Statutes.

For taxes, there is a slight increase in the amount of paper work, but no additional tax to pay. You are once again taxed individually on your 1040, but your partnership is required to submit form 1065 to the IRS. In North Carolina, your partnership is required to fill out form D-403. Even money that is earned by the partnership, yet held onto is taxed individually. This is important to note in case your company earns money for years without paying the owners. The owners are still liable for tax on that income.

The FICA tax is worth addressing, even though the outcome remains the same. The amount each partner earns is taxed at 7.65% (5.65% in 2012). A partner is deemed to have earned the income as soon as the partnership does regardless of if he or she receives any income, granted the net income of the partnership is only calculated at the end of the year. On top of the individual share, the partnership would have to pay 7.65% of all income. Since a partner is deemed to own only an equal share of the assets, profits and losses, this calculation looks very similar to the sole proprietorship.

As is similar to that of a sole proprietorship, there is unlimited liability for a partnership. This means that any debt or wrongdoing by one partner can cause the other partners to get sued personally. The partner or partners who get sued may always sue the wrongdoer for contribution to repay them, but that only works if the wrongdoer is able to be found and has enough money to cover the expense.

Limited Partnership (LP)

A limited partnership is similar to a partnership except the limited partners have no personal liability for the debts or actions of the partnership. Only the general partner or partners can be held personally liable; however, only the general partner or partners can manage the company. A general partner can be a corporation or LLC, but that asks the question: Why not just for an LLC or corporation?

With the advent of Limited Liability Companies, these Limited Partnerships have significantly decreased in numbers, since they require a filing with the state, retain some liability in the general partner, and are not as flexible with member/partner rights as an LLC.

Limited Liability Company (LLC)

This is, by far, the most popular choice recently in North Carolina, and we will spend a fair bit of time discussing why that is. The LLC isn't the best for all circumstances, but it is very flexible, tax neutral and has limited liability.

One of the most useful aspects of an LLC in North Carolina is the choice of how it is taxed. Because of the advantages of the partnership "pass-through" taxation, most choose that route so they are taxed only once as the income is earned. If you have an LLC with only one member, your LLC is treated as a disregarded entity for federal taxation purposes. This just means it is treated like a sole proprietorship instead of a partnership for taxation only. As a pass through entity, you will once again have to file form 1065 annually with the IRS and form D-403 for North Carolina. Each individual member will have to fill out his or her share on his or her 1040 and D-400. If the LLC is treated as a disregarded entity, everything will go on your individual 1040 and D-400.

For self-employment or FICA taxes, the taxes remain the same as if you were a sole proprietor for single member LLCs and the same as a partnership for pass through LLCs.

To form an LLC, you must file your articles of organization with the North Carolina Department of the Secretary of State and wait about a week for your certificate of organization in the mail. LLCs can have a name separate from its owners, so long as it does not contain any of the reserved words and it includes some variation or abbreviation of "limited liability company." It also cannot be the same name as another company in North Carolina, or suggest that the company performs a function that it does not. I could not name my law office "The Medical office of George Washington" because I do not perform medical services and I unfortunately cannot claim to be affiliated with George Washington. The cost for filing is $125 at the time I wrote this book. Once again, as with all entities, any business license must be obtained prior to starting business if one is required. With an LLC, you must also obtain an EIN from the IRS so that your company has a distinct identification number when opening bank accounts and filing taxes.

In order to maintain the LLC's active status, a few important formalities must be followed. First, an annual report must be filed every year with the state. This is a very simple form that asks for general information about your company and registered agent. Along with the annual report, you must also pay a $200 fee. The second formality is maintaining the distinct nature of the LLC. This means that you have to operate as though you were caring for someone else's stuff whenever you act, even if you're the only member. You can do this by writing letters authorizing you to do any action and signing as "managing member" or however your LLC treats management. You also must maintain separate bank accounts, having no comingling going on, ever. As soon as you use the business debit card to buy groceries, you put yourself at risk of ruining the limited liability nature of the LLC. Third, but not least, you must keep good records. All of your transactions and company decisions should be written down and stored. It may seem like a lot, but the formalities merely take getting used to. After that, they make a whole lot of sense, and they become second nature.

As long as you've followed the formalities and didn't do anything to bring liability on you personally, you will enjoy the limited liability of the LLC. No member automatically can be liable for the debts or wrongdoings of the LLC, its employees or its members. Furthermore, you can set up the LLC, fairly easily in fact, to ensure that if a member gets sued personally for an unrelated action that member's ownership interest cannot be taken in the lawsuit. This is a big difference between LLCs and Corporations where the stocks are assets available to the creditors. What the creditors can receive from the LLC is what is called a charging order, which only allows the creditor to receive income payments that would have gone to the member who got sued. The limited liability nature of an LLC is the biggest advantage it has over the general partnership or sole proprietorship, and it shares this advantage with S Corporations and C Corporations.

The LLC is owned by members and the ownership interest can be divided up however the members choose. Without an agreement otherwise, we would look to the North Carolina statutes to see who receives what interest amount. I would always recommend writing up an operating agreement when writing the articles of organization. Even a simple agreement goes a long way for resolving disputes down the road.

Another good part about LLCs is that membership can be bought, sold, traded, defined, inherited or transferred in nearly any other way. Since they are so flexible, you may also create different types of membership to create controlling and non-controlling members. This is beneficial if the members want to raise capital but do not want to give up any control of the company. If the investor will agree, it is a nice strategy to have available. Because they are so new, and because they cannot be traded on the stock market, many investors still shy away from LLCs, preferring the C Corporation instead.

S Corporation (S Corp)

An S Corporation is a corporation at the state level for all purpose except taxation. An S corporation is taxed just like a partnership, but only if it qualifies. To qualify, it must only have one class of stock, have on hundred or fewer shareholders, have no corporate or partnership shareholders, have only US citizens as shareholders, and the profits and losses must be proportional to each shareholder's interest in the company.

There are very few reasons to elect to be an S corporation because of the limited nature of the entity when compared to LLCs and C Corporations. That said, they're still listed here because there are times when an S Corporation is the best choice, and conversion between and S Corporation and a C Corporation is a very simple process.

C Corporation (C Corp)

The C corporation is the traditional vehicle for investment backed companies or companies with ever changing ownership. Although an LLC can operate in much the same way, the C Corp is more familiar and has the coveted "IPO."

To form a C corporation, you must file articles of incorporation with the North Carolina Department of the Secretary of State, file for an EIN through the IRS and pay the $125. At the time of formation, the shareholders must also elect board members to control the company and adopt bylaws to set the rules for how the company will operate.

C corporations are completely distinct from their owners. This means these entities are also taxed separately. Through the IRS, they must fill out form 1120, and in North Carolina, they fill out form CD-405. What is unpleasant about the C corporation is how distributions to the owners are taxed. Because dividends are not deductible, there is a "double tax" on the amount the corporation earns. First, that income is taxed at the corporate level when it is earned, but it is taxed again on the individual's 1040 as dividend income. Of course, you can pay workers a salary to avoid this double tax effect because wages are deductible from the corporate tax; however, wages must be paid reasonably for actual work done, and wages are taxed by FICA. Combine the individual income tax and the FICA together, and you'll generally have slight savings.

As with FICA, this is one entity where it is not going to

automatically be necessary to withhold FICA taxes. It is possible to have no earned income and only receive dividend income, which is not subject to FICA taxes. If you work for the corporation and receive wages, you will pay your 7.65% (5.65% in 2012) and the corporation will pay its 7.65% of your income.

With all the other entities, when the company earned income, the owners had to report the income on their 1040s regardless of if they were paid. Those other types of companies could not hold onto large amounts of cash without forcing their owners to pay tax on income they had not received. A corporation is taxed itself, so while it doesn't make distributions to its shareholders, its shareholders are not taxed. The saved money, however, can be taxed at the dividend rate if there is no legitimate reason to be storing up that money. This would lead to a "triple tax" situation, so it is best to ensure there is always a legitimate business reason when storing up money in the corporation.

The owners of a C corporation are the shareholders or stockholders. In a C corporation, shareholders can be people from any nation, companies, trusts or any other entity that is allowed to own assets in the United States. With no restrictions on who may own the shares, there is a much larger pool of potential investors available to a C corporation than to an S corporation, and with the stock markets, they are much easier to find than with an LLC.

The formalities of a C corporation are the strictest of all the choices. You must keep assets separate still. You must have bylaws and abide by them and the articles of incorporation. A C Corp must have an annual meeting of the shareholders where they may vote on things like new directors or changes to the bylaws. Meetings like the annual meeting must be recorded in meeting minutes, and an annual report must also be filed. If the C corporation wants to be publicly traded, there are significantly more formalities and filing obligations through the state of

North Carolina and through the SEC. Up until the point when you go public, these formalities, although rigid, are not too tough to follow. You're obligated to follow them, but they also help keep your company organized.

To provide a visual of what a corporation's governance looks like, the following hierarchy puts your company's documents in the order in which they take precedence over the others:

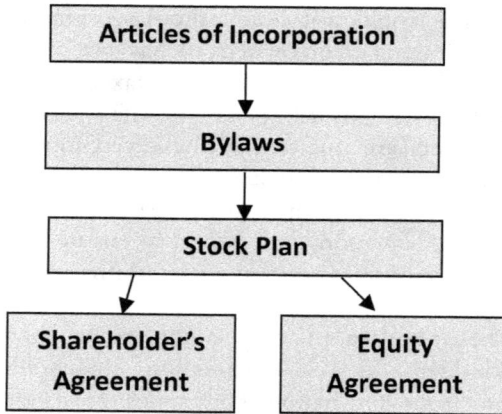

```
┌─────────────────────────────────┐
│     Articles of Incorporation   │
└─────────────────────────────────┘
                 │
                 ▼
┌─────────────────────────────────┐
│             Bylaws              │
└─────────────────────────────────┘
                 │
                 ▼
┌─────────────────────────────────┐
│           Stock Plan            │
└─────────────────────────────────┘
         │                 │
         ▼                 ▼
┌──────────────┐    ┌──────────────┐
│ Shareholder's│    │    Equity    │
│  Agreement   │    │  Agreement   │
└──────────────┘    └──────────────┘
```

CHAPTER 2
TREATMENT OF STARTUP FUNDS

Sometimes a small concept can make a huge difference. Because of the difference between Limited Liability Companies (LLCs) and Corporations, the money you put in to start them is treated in very different ways.

Overview of Corporations

A corporation is a distinct legal entity from the owners. It was created to separate management from ownership in order to lessen the legal liability of the owners. Owners hold onto a portion of the company in devices called shares. Shares do not need to by physical pieces of paper and are defined at the state level, usually by statute.

Ownership of a share or more than one share entitles a person to certain rights in the company, depending on the bylaws, stock purchase agreement or other contracts associated with the purchase or acquiring of the shares. Most shares come with the right to vote for the Board of Directors and on larger decisions, like whether or not to sell the company to a competitor or dissolve the company.

The Board of Directors in a corporation appoints the management of the company. The most iconic example of the management is the Chief Executive Officer, or CEO for short. The management then runs the day to day operations of the company.

Overview of LLCs

A limited liability company, or LLC for short, is a collection of owners (usually called members) acting together towards a common business purpose. The LLC is not distinct from the owners, but the LLC creates a limitation on personal liability just like the corporation does. LLCs were also created by statute and the rules for their operation are created under state law.

Under North Carolina law, since 2014, members are by default managers of the company. This can be changed in the LLC's operating agreement to have a single manager, group of managers, board of managers or any other setup that (1) has at least one manager, and (2) does not infringe on the guaranteed rights of the other members.

Tax Treatments

Disregarded – If a company is disregarded for tax purposes, it means there is only one owner, the company is not a corporation, and the company has not made some alternative tax election. This can only occur in sole proprietorships and single member LLCs. Companies taxed as disregarded entities report all income on the individual's 1040.

Partnership – If a company is tax as a partnership, it means that there are two or more owners, the company is not a corporation and the company has not elected to be taxed as a C or S corp. This can only occur in partnerships and multiple member LLCs. Companies taxed as partnership must send in a partnership tax return, issue K-1s to their owners and report the K-1 income on the owners' tax returns.

C Corporation – If a company is taxed as a C Corporation, it means that the company is either a corporation or an LLC. This is the default tax treatment of a corporation and able to be elected as an LLC. C Corporation taxation is the only type of taxation that has a separate tax rate for all business profit; however, salary to owners is considered a business expense, resulting in only income tax for all salaries paid to owners.

S Corporation – If a company is taxed as an S Corporation, it means that the company is either a corporation or an LLC and has elected to be taxed as an S Corporation. S Corporation election allows owners of a company to pay themselves a reasonable salary under partnership taxation rules and then pay themselves the remaining profit as distributions on equity, thereby saving the FICA taxes they would normally have to pay on ordinary income.

Startup Funds

Corporation – When you put money into a corporation, you are investing in exchange for shares. Generally, you only contribute money in exchange for new shares, but although not advisable, you can structure this different. Because you're exchanging money for shares, you can only recoup the money you've contributed when you dispose of the shares, either selling them to a third party or to the company. Any income you receive otherwise would be ordinary income or dividends in a corporation.

For example, if you contribute $100,000 for 100,000 shares, each share is worth $1. If you get paid $50,000 the first year, but retain all of your shares, you pay income tax on the $50,000. On the other hand, if you sell back 50,000 shares in exchange for $50,000, you will pay no taxes, as it will likely all be considered return on capital. If you sell back 10,000 shares in exchange for $50,000, a portion of the $40,000 gain would likely be considered capital gains instead of income for tax purposes and $10,000 would likely be considered return on capital. Be careful with this, however, because your company's valuation will affect these things. You cannot completely avoid income tax by trading your stock back, but if your company's value has increased significantly since you received your shares, it may be reasonable for the income to be capital gains opposed to income tax. Talk to a CPA or tax attorney before trying this later strategy.

Limited Liability Company – When you put money into an LLC, you are investing in exchange for equity. Under LLC taxation, this increases your capital account. When the LLC profits, you increase your capital account as well. You're subject to tax on only the amount you're liable for when the LLC profits, not when you're paid. This means that you will not be subject to certain taxes when getting paid because you're being paid above and beyond the profits.

For example, if you invest $100,000 in your LLC and you're the sole owner (100%), and your LLC makes $50,000 the first year. If you pay yourself $50,000, you pay income tax on the entire $50,000. If you pay yourself $60,000, you're only subject to income tax on the first $50,000 and the $10,000 would be return on capital.

Conclusion

LLCs can give you your return on capital faster as the company grows and is able to support itself whereas you must sell your shares of the corporation in order to take advantage of the return on capital tax treatment of corporate stock. These two different ways of handling taxation and investment may make the difference between forming a corporation or forming a limited liability company. There are many other factors, however, that you should be aware of.

CHAPTER 3
CORPORATION
FORMATION INTRO

To form your company, you will need to file the 'Articles' with the entity tasked with forming companies in your state. Each state is different, but in North Carolina, this is the Department of the Secretary of State. Fortunately, the NC Secretary of State's website includes Article templates that you can print and complete in order to complete your LLC Formation.

Suspension Reports
Verify Certification
Online Annual Reports
Print Forms

SEARCHES

Search By Corporate Name
Search For New & Dissolve

Corporation Article Parts

For your Corporation, there are a few required terms for your company's Articles of incorporation. The most common parts are:

Name of the Company. You name must include "Inc.," "Corporation," or any other common abbreviation for a Corporation or Incorporated. Before choosing a name, you should also run through a name search, checking the Secretary of State's site, the USPTO, register of deeds, Google, domain registry, and any state trademark offices in which you might want to conduct business.

Number of Shares. In North Carolina, there is no real formula for calculating how many shares you want to issue. This can also be changed in the future by filing Articles of Amendment. You do not have to issue all the shares right away, so what you should do is identify your plan for when you might issue shares and have enough to cover that, and no more. If you bring in an institutional investor, that investor will likely require that you change the number and class of shares, as well as initiate a stock plan for your company.

Classes of Shares. On the default Articles, provided by the Secretary of State, you're asked to select between your shares all being one class, called common stock, or having them divided into multiple classes of stock. If you select multiple classes of stock, you will have to add provisions that outline the rights, responsibilities, and numbers of each type of stock.

Some more frequently classified stock includes common stock and preferred stock. These are sometimes called voting and non-voting shares, although that is not an apt description of what they really are, though common stock generally is the voting stock and preferred stock is generally non-voting. You can also have things such as Common Stock A, B & C, which are just mildly different forms of stock.

All in all, what you call the stock is very unimportant. What is important is the rights and responsibilities you assign those share classifications. If you need help determining this, either speak with an attorney or look up examples from other companies that have multiple share types and hope they did it right.

Registered Agent and Address. This isn't required in all states, but it is the person or entity that is located within the state borders that is responsible for accepting service of process on behalf of the company. This is important because this is the place a person can sue a business in the event the business has wronged that person. Just by serving this person, even if the business owner never gets the lawsuit, subjects the business to the jurisdiction of the court.

Principal Office Location. This also isn't required in all states either, and it isn't required in North Carolina, but it provides a backup for the registered agent in case service cannot be obtained on the registered agent. It also provides the public with more information about your company.

Organizer. The Organizer does not necessarily have to be a Member, but the Organizer is the person who is setting up the LLC. This person has only the authority to set up the LLC, unless the Articles or Operating Agreement specify that she is a Member or Manager.

Other Provisions. Most corporations that either take public money through grants or government contracts, as well as corporations with institutional investors will want more provisions than what are required. You may want to consider other provisions when drafting your articles. Keep in mind that any change you make will cost you time and money, as you will have to file Articles of Correction or Articles of Amendment with the Secretary of State for every change.

In small companies, one of the most common added provisions is to list the owners. If you don't plan on changing owners that often, this is fine; however, if you're going to go through multiple rounds of financing or adding and removing owners, this would be a costly addition.

CHAPTER 4
STEP BY STEP
CORPORATION
FORMATION

We live in a DIY society, where everyone has some sort of do-it-yourself project going on somewhere. We find that when it comes to setting up your business, this still holds true. A lot of people we work with are setting up their own business structures with limited setback. Especially if you're on your own or have a very small company, this can have little to no risk.

We, of course, do not recommend doing this yourself, but if you're going to anyway, here are the steps you'd have to go through to get a properly set up Corporation in North Carolina. (Keep in mind there is a complex analysis around choosing between an LLC, Corporation or other type of legal entity. Choosing the wrong type may have unintended liability or tax consequences.)

Step 1: What is in a name?

A rose by any other name would smell as sweet, right? When you're picking your name, you may want to consult family, friends and branding experts to discuss what name or names would best fit your business idea. There are two general types of names: descriptive and creative. 'Google' is a good example of creative, and 'R. W. Bobholz Law, PLLC' is a good example of descriptive. As their names suggest, a descriptive name gives the audience a sense of what the company does whereas a creative name does not.

Step 2: Search for your name.

Once you've decided on a name, you're going to have to search the Secretary of State database to make sure the name isn't taken. Additionally, you should search the uspto.gov trademark database to ensure that you're not violating someone's trademark by using this name. Lastly, if you plan on having a website or any web presence, you should make sure that your domain name is available, preferably in a .com top level domain.

Secretary of State

Search: http://www.secretary.state.nc.us/corporations/csearch.aspx

Starting With   All words   Any words
Corporate Name Availability   Sounds Like
Exact Match   Sos Id   Only Active Corporations

Search

Search Page I

USPTO Trademark

Search:
http://tmsearch.uspto.gov/bin/gate.exe?f=tess&state=48
08:dnp1nt.1.1

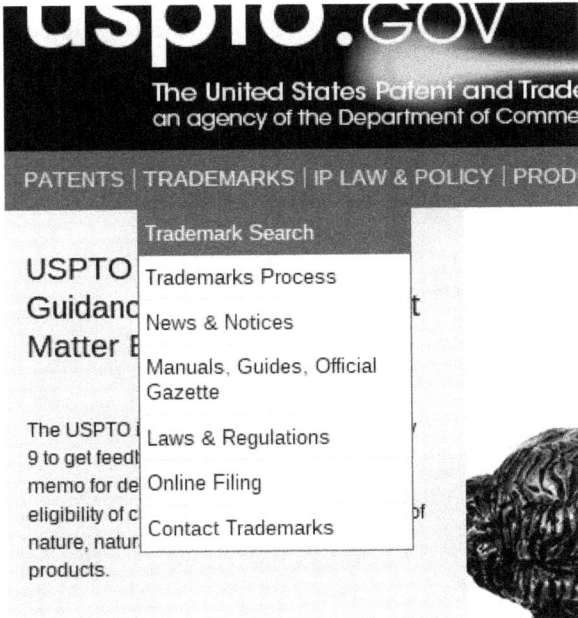

GoDaddy Domain

Search: http://www.godaddy.com/

Step 3: Download the Articles of Incorporation

In order to create a legal entity, you must file Articles of Incorporation with the Secretary of State's office here in North Carolina. This is an easy process that starts with downloading the empty Articles of Incorporation here: https://www.sosnc.gov/corporations/forms.aspx?PItemId=5465493&Type=BusinessCorporation

Step 4: Fill in the Articles

[Sample as of August 27, 2016 – Edited for Size and Formatting]

State of North Carolina
Department of the Secretary of State
Limited Liability Company
ARTICLES OF INCORPORATION

Pursuant to §55-2-02 of the General Statutes of North Carolina, the undersigned does hereby submit these Articles of Incorporation for the purpose of forming a business corporation.

1. The name of the corporation is: _____

2. The number of shares the corporation is authorized to issue is: _____

3. These shares shall be: *(check either a or b)*

a. ☐ All of one class, designated as common stock; or

b. ☐ Divided into classes or series within a class as provided in the attached schedule, with the information required by N.C.G.S. Section 55-6-01.

4. The name of the initial registered agent is:

_____

5. The North Carolina street address and county of the initial registered office of the corporation is:

Number and Street_____

City_____ State: NC Zip Code: _____

County:_____

6. The mailing address, *if different from the street address*, of the initial registered agent office is:

Number and Street_____

City_____ State: NC Zip Code: _____

County:_____

7. Principal office information: (*must select either a or b.*)

a. ☐ The corporation has a principal office.

The principal office telephone number:

_____

The street address and county of the principal office of the corporation is:

Number and Street_____

City_____ State: _____ Zip Code: _____
County:_____

    The mailing address, *if different from the street address*, of the principal office of the corporation is:

Number and Street_____
City_____ State: _____ Zip Code: _____
County:_____

    b. ☐ The corporation does not have a principal office

8. Any other provisions, which the corporation elects to include, i.e., the purpose of the corporation, are attached.

9. The name and address of each incorporator is as follows:

_____
_____
_____
_____

10. (Optional): Please provide a business e-mail address:

_____

The Secretary of State's Office will e-mail the business automatically at the address provided at no charge when a document is filed. The e-mail provided will not be viewable on the website. For more information on why this service is being offered, please see the instructions for this document.

11. These articles will be effective upon filing, unless a future date is specified:
This is the _____ day of _____, 20____.

_____

_____
Signature

_____
Type or Print Name and Title

You'll notice there are spots for Name of the Company, Number of Shares, Types of Shares, Name and Address of the Person Executing the Articles (aka "Incorporator"), Registered Agent, and office location. North Carolina makes forming an LLC very simple.

Name: Your name must be unique, not in violation of someone's trademark, not contain certain reserved words like engineer, lawyer, architect, etc. without board approval, and must contain some variation or abbreviation of "limited liability company."

Number of Shares. The only requirement to this is there must be at least 1 share. If you do enough digging around on the Secretary of State's website, you'll find plenty of corporations that have issued only 1 share.

Classes of Shares. Unless you have a compelling reason otherwise, you should almost always choose the first option "All of one class, designated as common stock." One general rule here is to not get creative. The more creative you get, the less likely your Articles will be effective, or even valid. I have, in fact, seen Articles filed without any classes of shares able to vote to change the Articles. This is the area of the Articles that is the easiest to make a mistake that can cost you greatly.

Registered Agent: Your registered agent is responsible for receiving important documents from the state or potential claimants on behalf of your company. This can be you, but whoever it is must be a resident or company physically located in this state and have an address that is not a PO Box.

Office: Your company is not required to have an office; however, if it does have a principal office in this state, it must be recorded here. If you do not have an office, check the line that says this company does not have a principal office.

Incorporator: Here, you will need a natural person or company that is actually filling out the form. This will likely be you, another member of your company or your attorney. You will also need the address. Keep in mind that every Incorporator listed will have to sign these Articles. It is usually best to only have one.

Signatures: If your Incorporator is a natural person (not a company), you should sign as a natural person in the bottom. If this is a company, you'll sign as a company by putting the company name on top, your signature in the middle and printing your name below the signature. This signature area must match the section that requires the Incorporator's information, and they will get rejected if you list a natural person as Incorporator and sign as a company or vice versa.

Once you fill out all of the information, you'll need print this form off and have the Incorporator sign it. You will then scan this signed document in as a pdf and save to your computer in an area easy to remember.

Step 5: Sign up for an online account on North Carolina's Secretary of State page

You can mail in, hand deliver, or submit your Articles of Incorporation online through the online system. Hand delivery is the only way to get 4-hour return service; however, absent the need for extremely rapid turnaround, the best option, in my opinion, is the online system. It costs $2, and allows you to make changes to the Articles in case there are mistakes without having to wait for the returned mail. It is also very fast. If there isn't a backlog, you will typically receive a response within a few days. (No promise though, as the Secretary of State can take weeks to reply to your submission, if need be.)

To sign up, first visit here:
http://www.secretary.state.nc.us/corporations/

The form is simple:

E-Account Information

Is this a business entity: ☟
Yes ▼

Entity Name:

Address:

City:	State:	Zip Code:	Country:
	NC ▼		USA ▼

Telephone Number: ☟   **Contact E-Mail:** ☟

Notification E-Mail: ☟   **Billing E-Mail:** ☟

Account Name: ☟

Password: ☟   **Verify Password:** ☟

Industry: ☟
▼

Enable ACH: ☟
No ▼

Keep in mind that your entity name should not be the corporation you are about to file because it doesn't exist yet. Instead, make the entity name your name. Once you fill out the form and submit, you're automatically logged into your account.

Step 6: Upload a Creation Filing

From here, you will go to "Upload a Creation Filing" on the left menu bar. This will bring you to another form to be filled out. This form requires you to include the new company's name, type and document type. There should be only one option for document type.

After inputting all of these fields, you must also upload the saved pdf by choosing the file and then clicking upload.

The next screen will show a list of the filings you have in process. You should only have one selection. Click on the radio button next to it, ensure the information in the following fields are correct and then click "Pay & Submit"

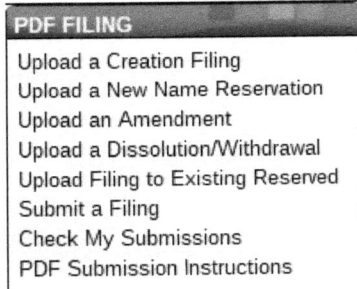

PDF FILING

Upload a Creation Filing
Upload a New Name Reservation
Upload an Amendment
Upload a Dissolution/Withdrawal
Upload Filing to Existing Reserved
Submit a Filing
Check My Submissions
PDF Submission Instructions

Step 7: Pay

On the payment page, you need to fill out the payment information and click through the page. Once payment is received and processed, you will receive notification on the next page. You must then wait until the Secretary of State's office follows up with you regarding any changes that must be made or if the articles are accepted.

Step 8: Make and Submit any Changes

If the articles are rejected, they will be rejected with a reason attached. You will then be able to make the necessary changes and resubmit the articles. This is the major advantage to using the online version because you can email back and forth with the individual assigned to your filing until you have the Articles of Incorporation correct, at no additional charge.

CHAPTER 5
STEPS AFTER ARTICLES
ARE APPROVED

So, you received your approved Articles of Organization or Incorporation from the Secretary of State? Congratulations. That's a huge, tangible, first step to becoming a well-protected company. The next few steps are also very important, but you can take care of them pretty quickly immediately afterwards.

EIN

The first step after approval is getting your Employer Identification Number (EIN). If you're obtaining this yourself, you can do the entire process online and get your EIN in about 5 minutes. You'll need your approved articles and information about yourself like your social security number.

The EIN isn't just for companies that have employees. It is not a very good name for it. A more appropriate name would be tax ID number. It is your company's equivalent of a social security number. All the company's tax and banking records will be tied to this EIN.

We've create a nice walkthrough that you can use when

completing your online EIN application. There is no charge, and the process is very quick. Do not pay someone to do this for you unless it is just included in other services. We cover this portion in the next chapter.

Governing Document

Every LLC and Corporation is required to have a governing document; however, LLCs have a default one set by the General Assembly. The terms North Carolina has set are fine for single member LLCs, but when you're a multimember LLC or a corporation of any size, you should create a governing document that meets your company's needs.

An LLC would have an operating agreement, which covers how the company is run, but also how the members interact with each other. Since an LLC is a collection of members, most of the document revolves around the members.

A corporation has bylaws. These are the rules that the management must follow when operating the business. A corporation is a separate legal entity and the roles are far clearer than with an LLC. Because of this distinction, you see very little about owners' rights and responsibilities and more about management. Bylaws are usually accompanied by some form of equity agreement, stock purchase agreement, and/or stock plan to better define the owners' rights and responsibilities.

Your articles will always supersede your governing document, so be sure to not try to override anything you put in those articles.

Bank Account

Every company should have its own bank account. Otherwise, you could risk personal liability for all the company's debts, and that defeats the purpose of setting up the company in the first place. Usually, a bank will need your approved articles, EIN, governing document, and identification in order to open your account. Our advice would be to find a bank that you trust and use them, but it does not hurt to shop around for the bank that best serves your needs.

Articles and Organization

Although you can always access your articles online at the Secretary of State's website, your approval cover page won't be available there. We recommend scanning your approved articles to a place you store important records and keep them in a binder or safe with your EIN, bank account information, and your governing document. Keeping all of this stuff in one place helps ensure you can access it when you need to.

CHAPTER 6
OBTAIN AN EIN

After your Articles of Incorporation are accepted by the Secretary of State, the next step in the company startup process is to apply for an Employee Identification Number (EIN) from the IRS.

Filing for an EIN is a fairly simple process that takes about 5 minutes to complete. The IRS has made a question and answer program on their site that guides you through the process. Even though the process is simple, don't rush through any parts because fixing an EIN error after the fact is far more difficult than applying for one in the first place.

The online application can be found here: http://www.irs.gov/Businesses/Small-Businesses-&-Self-Employed/Apply-for-an-Employer-Identification-Number-(EIN)-Online

Note: Although it is online, the ability to file for an EIN is only available between the hours of 7am and 10pm Eastern time. Bizarre? Maybe.

To begin, click the button at the bottom that reads Apply Online Now.

Step 1

The first thing they want to know is what type of business. For the sake of an easy to understand guide, we're forming a Corporation here.

Step 2

Following our example, the next page asks what type of corporation. Almost every corporation is going to select the first option, which is just "Corporation" again.

Step 3

The next input page asks why you need an EIN. Typically, this is because you've started a new business, but be sure to check the appropriate button.

Step 4

The next page asks about the responsible party. This is you if you're filing for the EIN. Go ahead and click individual if you're applying as a natural person. The next page will ask your personal information, name and social security number. It will also ask how you are the responsible party. If you're not an owner, member or manager, you will have to do a few extra steps. (Need an SS-4 and Form 2848 on record in your files in case of audit)

Step 5

The next step asks for information about the Corporation's physical location. Even if the Corporation does not have an office, you need to fill out this portion. You may have to use your home address or the address of your registered agent (if permissible by your agent) if you do not have a business address.

Step 6

After that page, we finally get to the meat of the business. This page asks for information on the Corporation, like name and location. The IRS asks for the state the company was formed as well as state the company is located. These can be different, so that's why both are asked.

Tip: You cannot include most punctuation marks in the name or address fields anywhere in this application.

Step 7

The Page after that contains what I refer to as the red flag items. Most companies will click 'no' for all of these, but be sure to read through them carefully. Clicking yes may yield more work through this process, however. Lying on any of these can be incredibly problematic. Just don't lie.

Step 8

Then, you must select what your business does. On most categories, there will be a subcategory on the following page as well. Select the category that best describes your business and move on. 'Other' is actually a very commonly used selection, so don't worry if you don't see something that fits exactly.

Tip: 'Service' is a subcategory of 'Other'.

Step 9

At this point, you're done inputting information. Just read through the next couple of pages and be sure to print off the confirmation letter that you receive, if you choose to receive this online.

Step 10

If you've done everything correct, you'll likely have an EIN by the end of this process. If there were any errors, and the IRS does not provide any feedback on why the error was received, you may either want to start over or seek help.

Keep in mind to check the time if you receive an error. It may be too late to receive an EIN, even if the service let you start the application. I wouldn't recommend starting an application after 9:45pm Eastern Time.

Tip: If someone previously registered a company with the same name in your state, you will have an error and have to call the IRS, even if that previous company is dissolved.

Step 11

Print off or capture a screenshot of the EIN. If you were obtaining this EIN for yourself, or your own company where you are the responsible party, you will be able to print off the EIN letter. If you are not the responsible party, you will have to wait 4-8 weeks for this letter to arrive in the mail.

CHAPTER 7
WHAT'S IN A
CORPORATION'S BYLAWS

Bylaws are the governing documents for Corporations. In the bylaws, you would specify things from how meetings are conducted to what director and officer positions exist within the company. This is one of your most important documents a corporation will have. Bylaws are usually coupled with some form of stock plan, shareholder agreement, or other type of equity agreement to define the rights and responsibilities of the shareholders.

Most shareholder rights and responsibilities are not included in the bylaws because the bylaws focus on governance rather than ownership principles. Over the next couple of chapters, we'll be looking at the governance of the Corporation.

Technically, all corporations are required to have bylaws; however, the bylaws do not need to be that complicated when it is owned by a single shareholder. The bylaws are still important to have because it is one of the formalities required when establishing your limited personal liability for a corporation.

This chapter will only outline the most common terms in the Bylaws, but the possibilities are as expansive as your mind.

Definitions

You've probably seen this in statutes, contracts and all sorts of legal documents, so the Bylaws are no different. Since it is such a controlling document, it is important that every officer, director, investor, and shareholder is clear on what a term means. The bylaws are only as effective as they are clear; therefore, this is one of the more important sections when interpreting all the other parts of the document.

Ownership

The ownership terms are probably the ones most cared about by the shareholders, yet should be the simplest term in the entire document. Somewhere in your bylaws, there should be a mechanism for recording who owns what shares and what types of shares.

Board of Directors

Corporations are run by boards. This is part of what gives corporations the limited personal liability. Because there is a clear separation between ownership and management, the legal system many centuries ago decided that we could not hold the shareholders responsible for acts of the corporation.

In the Board of Directors section, you will want to define how many directors the corporation has, how the directors are added or removed, any qualifications or salary for directors, conflict of interest policies, and any board positions (like secretary) or committees the board may have.

Officers

Your Board of Directors generally has one major duty, and that is to appoint the management of the company. The management is commonly known as the officers of the corporation. The positions of CEO, President, Vice President, CFO, COO, etc. are all officer positions. These can be defined however you'd like, but it is important to ensure that all the powers of running the company are ultimately passed onto the officers.

In this section, you'll want to outline what the officer positions are, how they're appointed or removed, any rights and responsibilities that they have, any qualifications they must have, and any restrictions you want to place on their ability to act.

This is another section where getting too creative can hurt you. There's nothing wrong with saying there is one officer, the President, and that officer is appointed by the Board to carry out all tasks necessary to run the company. That's the simplest form of officer structure.

I've actually seen corporations that have created a system of officers that prevent anything from getting done in a corporation because of the recursive nature of their authority. If the CEO cannot act without the COO's permission who cannot act without the CFO's permission, and the CFO cannot act without the CEO's permission, that's a great way to stall your company.

Meetings

Corporations are known for their meetings, although LLCs should be conducting as many meetings as the corporation for organizational sake.

At a minimum, corporations are required to have an annual meeting where the shareholders get to appoint the Board of Directors. Something to that effect should be in your bylaws. On top of that, you will want to create types of meetings for important matters, like board meetings or special meetings for things like acquisition offers. Your bylaws will specify how and why these meetings can be called, any notice requirements, what quorum is, and how the meetings are run.

Transfer of Shares

Although this is more appropriately placed in a share plan or shareholder's agreement, you can specify how and why shares can be transferred or any limitations on the transferability of shares.

This is an area that, if not done right, can either be unenforceable, or can leave open violations of SEC laws. In smaller corporations, this is an area that isn't incredibly necessary to be addressed. Transfers of shares can also upset any tax election your company may have made.

Taxation Options

There are numerous tax sections that can be utilized when starting a small business. In order to take advantage of these provisions, your company must elect to do so, in many cases. Therefore, it is important to make that election and the requirements to obtain that election be clearly stated in the Bylaws.

Record Keeping

The larger the company, the bigger record keeping becomes. Records are the memory of the company, so it is important to keep the records in a manner that others can comprehend. To do this, you need to be organized from the start. One good way of being organized is requiring general practices in your Bylaws. Getting audited is bad enough, but getting audited when you have poor record keeping methods could be costly.

Corporations are required to keep minutes of their meetings. This is for your limited personal liability protection as well as for good institutional memory.

Dissolution

Companies close down. It happens, and when it does, it is important to have a plan in place on how to sell off assets or distribute assets to the shareholders. The last thing a failing company wants is to have the shareholders suing each other and the company over who gets which assets.

Dividends

If your company is going to distribute dividends, put in the bylaws how these are decided and on what date a person qualifies to receive the dividends. Most smaller corporations will not ever give dividends because the tax treatment isn't beneficial to small corporations, but if you do, keep these things in mind.

Other General Provisions

Other sections will be needed depending on the nature of the company. If it isn't already mentioned in the Articles of Incorporation, it would be useful to outline how to amend or modify the Bylaws and the purpose of the company.

CHAPTER 8
SHAREHOLDER
AGREEMENTS

Last chapter focused on the general provisions found in the bylaws. This chapter will focus more on shareholder provisions found in a stock plan or shareholder's agreements. For the sake of simplicity, we're using the term "shareholder's agreements" to mean all types of agreements between a company and a shareholder that outline the rights and responsibilities of shareholders, as well as number of shares. We're not using this term to mean the stock plan which is an umbrella to the shareholder agreements. Stock options, convertible debt, and other more sophisticated shareholder agreements are included in our definition of shareholder agreements, but we do not go into much detail about them specifically in this book.

Keep in mind that companies vary wildly in their operation, so the terms that are important to you might not be the same terms that are important to others. You want to be very thorough with this document and be sure that it covers everything that you need it to and says none of the things you do not want it to. Mishaps in this document can cause costly problems if not able to be resolved peacefully.

Depending on your company, you may want a stock

plan and shareholder's agreement, or rely solely on shareholder agreements to cover these rights and responsibilities. It is your choice, but from our diagram earlier, you'll see that the share plan offers a higher authority than individual shareholder agreements when structuring your company ownership. If you do use both a share plan and the shareholder's agreement, you should reference the share plan in the shareholder's agreement as a binding instrument to anyone signing the shareholder's agreement.

Division of Ownership

You'll find that shareholders really like to focus their attention on two things: How much do I own, and how will I get paid? Because of how important these things are, they should be very clear in your agreements. Fortunately, corporations are easy to divide ownership. Shares are something we all understand.

If I have 100 share of a corporation, I have 100 shares. That makes sense.

Dilution

After a shareholder knows how much they own, they will want to know how much they own compared to everyone else. 100 shares of a 1,000 share company are vastly different than 100 shares of a one billion share company.

Your Articles contain the number of total shares eligible to be issued; however, they rarely contain any policies or procedures to how they're issued or how the company can request more shares to be issued.

If you have a stock plan, the limitations on how shares can be issued and how more shares can be created will be in there. Otherwise, that information will likely have to be kept in the bylaws of the company. The reason it is not in the shareholder agreements is because those are likely different for each shareholder, and each individual shareholder will not be liable to follow every single shareholder agreement the company signs. The stock plan is a contract between the company and every shareholder.

Note: There are companies that have multiple stock plans, and that is fine, as long as they do not overlap. Each stock plan covers a different set of shares. For example, you can have a stock plan that covers 20,000 stocks reserved for an employee stock option pool.

Instead of using shareholder agreements, we rely on the share plan for outlining under what circumstances the company is permitted to issue more stock, redeem issued stock, create new stock, or do anything that would dilute or inflate any shareholder's ownership in the company.

In the stock plan, you want to include very clear language as to how shares can be issued, redeemed, created, or destroyed. You should also include how these shares are recorded.

Voting/Non-Voting

It shouldn't be surprising that shareholders want to know if they get to vote, how they vote, and what they get to vote on. The default is that owners of common shares get to vote on appointing the board of directors. That, however, shouldn't be the only thing they can vote on. You should consider what corporate events you would want your shareholders to vote on, like dissolution, mergers, acquisitions, issuance of new shares, and more. This kind of information should be included in your Articles, but if it is not, definitely include it in your share plan. To determine what class an individual shareholder owns, the shareholder agreement would specify what class of stock that shareholder has.

What to do in Case of Disagreements

Owners in a company disagree. It happens to every company, no matter how close the owners are. The important thing is to ensure that when the disagreements come up, there are clear rules in your governing documents as to how to deal with them. These rules can vary wildly from a coin flip to a forced sale of the company, but the most important thing is that the way the disagreement is settled is fair. To be fair, it must be clear and it must be established prior to any disagreement or ill will. If the policy is unfair or created after disagreements start, it will give the appearance of one of the owners trying to cheat the others, and therefore, can actually lead to larger problems than just the disagreement.

The key is to create policies that settle disputes when the waters are calm. Once the waters are choppy, the disagreement provisions are important, but agreeing on them without a mediator will be difficult and can lead to larger problems.

In corporations, these dispute settlement provisions are somewhat tricky. In a small corporation with only a couple owners, you can put it in the bylaws without any issue; however, when you get to corporations that have owners with different classes of shares and wildly varying numbers of shares, you do not want to have the same dispute resolution policy for every shareholder.

Think about what rights are fair when having a dispute with the corporation. Also bear in mind that minority shareholders have extra rights when corporations take actions that are detrimental to the minority shareholder's interest in the company. These minority shareholder rights vary state to state, but ultimately, they assign the board a duty of care when affecting a minority shareholder.

Buyback Provisions

There are good and bad reasons to have a buyback provision in your shareholder agreements or share plan. A buyback provision is a clause in your shareholder agreements, bylaws, or stock plan that allows the company or a majority shareholder to buy other shareholder's share at a specific time or upon the occurrence of a specific event. Usually buyback provisions also include a specific price or a formula to calculate the price to make the buyback process more predictable.

Buyback provisions are common when the investment into the company is structured more like a loan or in earlier rounds of investment. Upon a certain event (many times a larger investment), the shares with the buyback provision are reacquired by the company with a profit built into them for the shareholders who are surrendering their shares.

These provisions can be requested by the shareholder when the shareholders are investors, but most times, they're included to protect the majority shareholder's interest in the company. It is in this circumstance that you need to be careful. As discussed before, minority shareholders do have certain rights when it comes to the duty owed to them. You also have to be careful of illusory contracts or failure to meet the requirements of deferred compensation laws when you structure these types of deals.

The great thing about buyback provisions is the flexibility they give you for IPOs or future investment. These are the best circumstances to use it, but there are many situations where the provision may be required.

Transferability of Shares

There are dozens of reasons why you would want to limit the ability of your shareholders to transfer their shares. From preventing a hostile corporate takeover to complying with SEC regulations, the reasons for limiting transferability of shares varies wildly. Some restrictions are to prevent the company from violating the law whereas others are for business reasons.

You can limit the transfer of shares in most cases, but you have to be careful when limiting it, especially in involuntary transfers like bankruptcy, death, or liens of creditors.

In some circumstances, like involuntary transfers, it may be a good idea to have a right of first refusal instead of an absolute restriction. The right of first refusal gives the company or the other shareholders the right to purchase the shares at a defined value or the value assigned in certain proceedings before the shares can be transferred. If those with that right pass on it, cannot afford it, or fail to act, only then do the shares transfer to the third party.

Right of first refusal is one of those win-win-win situations if done correctly. A creditor would much rather have cash than the shares of a corporation, but they only want cash when they get the value that should be assigned to them. This right of first refusal prevents a third party from entering your business, protects the creditor's right, and gives the original shareholder some protections when it comes to transferring and ownership responsibilities.

Vesting and Lockup

There are a lot of more specific rights and terms you can add to share ownership. One of these is called "vesting" where shares only become owned by the shareholder upon the happening of certain events or the passage of time. Vesting is incredibly helpful especially when a person is granted shares in exchange for labor or investments over time.

The vesting provision helps ensure that the shareholder isn't granted the full amount of shares without doing the full amount of work. Although there are contractual protections that can allow the company to seek damages or return of some shares from the shareholder for not performing, it is far easier to simply not grant the shares to that shareholder in the first place.

Vesting provisions are almost always in the specific shareholder's agreement because they can and should vary from shareholder to shareholder. It wouldn't make sense to have someone who already contributed all the value or labor to the company to be on the same vesting schedule as someone who is contributing work over several years.

A lockup period is another fairly specific clause that can be included in a share plan or a shareholder's agreement. A lockup period is incredibly specific as it only applies in the event of an initial public offering or a merger or acquisition. The lockup period is a specified length of time before and/or after one of these events that shareholders are not permitted to buy, sell, or transfer their shares in the company. This is to prevent insider trading or intentional manipulation of the markets.

Restrictive Legends

Restrictive legends are a must-have in any shareholder agreement. Basically, these are the bold-faced legal protection for the company when selling or assigning shares. There is specific language that you can get from a securities attorney or the SEC (including your state's Securities Division) that you should include. Essentially, these state that the shares are acquired for investment purposes, that there weren't other promises, and the specific SEC classification for the shares.

If there were any promises or any investment details given, this information should be explained in the restrictive legend portion as well. These restrictive legends should be on each shareholder agreement.

IPO Considerations

IPO is many times the dream of a corporation. If an initial public offering is the exit strategy for your company, corporation is the only company structure that will get you there. Just having a corporation, however, is not enough. You must also plan for the IPO.

We've already discussed lockup periods and buyback provisions. Both of these are fairly common when an IPO is likely. There are other provisions that you would likely consider including in your bylaws, your share plan, and your shareholder agreements if this is your direction.

Firstly, you need to establish what input shareholders have when considering an IPO. Do you want them to be able to vote or have it a board decision? If they can vote, what percent vote is required to make that decision?

Secondly, on what date will all buying and selling of shares have to cease?

Thirdly, there cannot still be common vesting of shares after an IPO. There can still be stock options vesting, but not ordinary shares. If you have that, you should include language that determines how those shares are handled. You can choose to cut off all vesting, make them vest automatically at a specific date, or convert them into some other type of deferred compensation.

If IPO is your exit plan, a DIY structure of governing documents will not suffice, and you should talk to an experienced securities attorney and CPA regarding your plan.

Dissolution or Acquisition

I always like to consider acquisitions and mergers along the same line as IPO. There are less legal requirements in these; however, you should still be considering the same things. The reasons behind no longer being able to vest shares in an IPO still exists for a merger or acquisition, but instead of being required by the federal government, they're required by function of the transaction.

In any merger, acquisition, or dissolution, you need to consider how much input the shareholders have. Once again, do you want the vote to go to the shareholders and what percent is required to pass?

Ultimately, when structuring any shareholder agreement or stock plan, you need to think through what would happen if there were a merger, an acquisition, a spin-off company, a dissolution, or an IPO at any stage in the company's existence. These are all very company-changing events that can impact everyone's interest in the company.

In dissolutions, specifically, you need to know and outline what happens to the company assets and in what order people get paid. Let's say there's $500,000 in assets, $350,000 in liabilities. Who gets the other $150,000? Is it spread prorated? Does it all go to a specific type of stock? These are important questions.

In an acquisition, similar questions present themselves. You've sold the company, so who gets paid what? Do all shareholders have to sell their shares in a company purchase? Is the company allowed to sell all or virtually all of the company assets in an asset purchase structured sale?

Frequently, there are two types of stock used in growth companies: Common and Preferred. Whereas common stock gets to vote on most matters, preferred stock gets paid first in an acquisition or dissolution up to the value of their shares, and sometimes including a little profit.

This difference between common and preferred (or other types of shares) should be clearly outlined in your Articles with more in depth descriptions and plans in your bylaws and share plan.

CHAPTER 9
CHECK MARK STARTUP

This book was very narrowly tailored to the legal side of forming a Corporation in North Carolina. Although it contains a lot of great information about that process, this is only a tiny fraction of the things you need to consider when starting your own business.

Check Mark Startup is a fantastic book by Richard Wayne Bobholz about taking your values and an idea and turning it into a strong business. The process can take as little as a week and saves business owners time, money, and stress while ensuring their business is on a solid legal and business foundation.

Richard wrote Check Mark Startup using real world experiences in his own business and the businesses of over 100 entrepreneurs. The goal wasn't to create a book about theories or new practices in starting up a business. Instead, the book was designed to help you create the well-oiled machine that allows for the rapid growth of your new company. Using these systems, you can easily move onto the next step or outsource any aspect of your business.

The real beauty of Check Mark Startup is the simplicity of each step. Richard requires the reader to know very little about business or law in order to jump in and create their own business from scratch. Built for beginners and experts alike, this book is a must have for any entrepreneur.

What could take you years to figure out, Richard has

outlined to ensure you discover within the first couple of months of starting your business. Check Mark Startup is comprehensive in its efforts to help you build systems that allow you to setup and forget. This allows you to be able to move on to the growth efforts of your company. Systems, like the ones in Check Mark Startup, add immense value to your company, both in sale value and in growth potential.

Check Mark Startup is available on Amazon.com. To find out more and get special tips, tricks, and promotions, check out www.checkmarkstartup.com.

ABOUT THE AUTHOR

Richard Bobholz is an award-winning attorney, speaker, business owner, teacher, and dedicated community member. He is the author of several other books in the business and science fiction genres, focusing his more recent publications on business, legal, and computer programming. Beyond helping his community through these resources, Richard dedicates a significant amount of his time to providing community service and pro bono legal services to the less fortunate in his community.

Richard enjoys running, backpacking, computer programming, writing, and spending time with family and friends.

Richard obtained his Bachelor's Degree in Economics at Michigan Technological University and his Juris Doctorate from the Kline School of Law at Drexel University.

Richard currently practices at Law Plus Plus, a revolutionary and award-winning law firm that is dedicated to making the legal system easier, enacting positive change in the community, and constantly improving how they operate and the effect they have on their clients' lives and in their profession. With this mission and his genuine approach to the practice of law, he is able to help small businesses, nonprofits, and social entrepreneurs protect themselves and develop their businesses in a deliberate and systematic manner.

Above the degrees and accolades, Richard values his ability to see things from multiple perspectives. This view of the world helps him break down problems into their simplest components and build a solution from that analysis. It is this style of thinking that allows him to create such useful books and guides, and is an incredibly valuable resource for his clients.

In 2015, Law Plus Plus was recognized by the American Bar Association for their contribution to pro bono services, taking second place nationwide for their commitment, and in 2016, Law Plus Plus became the first law firm in North Carolina to become B Corporation Certified.

Beyond those accomplishments, the attorneys at Law Plus Plus also contribute hundreds of hours every year toward community service through programs like Habitat for Humanity, Clean Jordan Lake, the Food Bank, Activate Good and so many more.

Richard also sits on the Board of Trustees for Activate Good, an amazing organization that promotes and pairs volunteers with causes, creating a multiplier effect in the community. The organization not only supports these nonprofits, but also inspires the next generation of leaders through their Activate Schools program and gives the resources needed to get businesses involved in coordinated days of service for their employees.